Inspira

366 Uplifting Thoughts & Quotations

Adele & Garry Malone

In Memory
of
Kim Buckley

Inspirations

366 Uplifting Thoughts & Quotations

Adele & Garry Malone

Tranceformational Publications
Tel/Fax: 01923 245181 email: garry.malone@virgin.net

Tranceformational Publications

2 Talbot Avenue Watford Herts WD1 4AX
Tel\Fax: 01923 245181 email: garry.malone@virgin.net

First Published in the UK
by Tranceformational Publications in January 1999

A Catalogue record for this book
is available from the British Library

ISBN 0 9533064 0 2

Printed and bound in Great Britain by
Antony Rowe Ltd, Chippenham, Wiltshire

ACKNOWLEDGEMENTS

.Every effort has been made to acknowledge all the source material and to secure permission
from copyright holders when required. In the event of any question arising as to the source of
any material we will be pleased to make the necessary acknowledgement in future printing.

SPECIAL ACKNOWLEDGEMENT AND THANKS

To our four wonderful children Molly, Harriette-Rose, Charlotte and Garry.
We love you, thank you for your unconditional love, support and inspiration.

Special Note To The Reader

Inspirations contains many uplifting thoughts and quotations that date back hundreds and in some cases even thousands of years. They have been reproduced in their original format. Please do not be offended by the use of the word 'man' instead of 'women' in many of the quotations. In the context of this book the word 'man' is used in the generic form and represents both men and women alike. If you feel you need to, simply replace the word man with women.

Other Titles by Adele & Garry Malone

Books with Free CD's.

The Essence of Reiki - a complete guide to first & second degree.
ISBN 0 9532620 0 6

The Greatest Love of All - stress management for the soul.
ISBN 0 9533064 1 0

Other Titles by Garry Malone

Audio Books

Stop Smoking Start Living   ISBN 0 9532620 2 2

Tranceformational Meditations   ISBN 0 9532620 1 4

INTRODUCTION

A few simple words in the form of an uplifting quotation or thought can often bring comfort, direction and inspiration into a person's life. *Inspirations* is a collection of words of wisdom from many of the great thinkers and leaders from the past and present day.

There is a new consciousness sweeping our planet. People are becoming more emotionally and spiritually aware. In a world that is developing at an unfathomable pace, it is important to take a few moments each day to develop your own path.

Life is the most precious gift of all. We are all here to love, learn and grow. Use this book to unlock your own path so you can achieve your full potential and destiny.

We are all special. We all possess a special gift or talent that needs to be expressed. Daily meditation will lead to enlightenment and fulfilment. Life is meant to be an adventure, not a bore. Take charge of your life, set your own path to follow, and you will open the door to a new and better life, filled with excitement, opportunity, self fulfilment and love.

Welcome To The Adventure

Adele & Garry Malone

Words of Wisdom
for the mind body & soul

HOW TO USE THIS BOOK

TODAY'S DATE

1) Open the book at today's date.

2) Read the quote or uplifting thought aloud several times.

3) Using 'The Enlightenment Meditation' on the free CD Inspirational meditations, spend a few moments meditating on the meaning and message that today's words of wisdom holds for you. Often at a deeper and more relaxed level you will be amazed at how a few simple words can bring greater meaning, depth and confidence into your life.

4) If it is inconvenient to play the CD and meditate on any particular day, spend a few moments thinking of how these words of wisdom could be incorporated into your life. Write down the words on a blank sheet of paper and repeat them aloud. This simple technique known as mind mapping will lead to an abundance of additional thoughts, ideas, associations, images and emotions. Write them all down in the form of pictures or words. You can also carry the piece of paper around with you and work on it during the day when you have a few spare moments. The ideas and messages that are developed as a result of this method are often incredible and truly inspiring.

PICK A DATE AT RANDOM

1) Think of a date at random. It could be a birthday, an anniversary, a future engagement or appointment or simply the first date that comes to mind. *Then repeat steps 2-4 as shown on previous page.*

DIP IN AT RANDOM

1) Open the book at random and focus on the quote or uplifting thought that you are first drawn towards. *Then repeat steps 2-4 as shown on previous page.*

ASK FOR GUIDANCE AND INSPIRATION

1) Place the book between the palms of your hands. Depending on what is happening in your life at any given moment, ask the book for guidance and inspiration to help overcome any challenges or daily setbacks. This is done by asking a simple and relevant question to the book and asking for an answer.
Once you have asked the question, open the book at the page you are drawn towards. This powerful technique often brings amazing and profound results. *Then repeat steps 2-4 as shown on previous page.*

GROUP MEETINGS

The techniques on the previous two pages can also be used in the following group settings as a source of fun, amusement, group planning and goal setting:

1) With your family.

2) Parties and social gatherings.

3) Company sales or motivational meetings. You can adopt a quote for the day, week, month, quarter or year and build a meeting or company promotion around it. There is always lots to discuss as the quote or uplifting thought will mean different things to different people.

4) In a classroom/teaching/ workshop environment.

USE YOUR IMAGINATION

Finally, why not try and develop your own unique ways of using the book. If you do come up with a new way of using this book and free CD and would like to share your idea with us, so we can include it in future printings please write, fax or email us and if we can use it we will be sure to acknowledge you as the source.

Ideas & Notes

HOW TO USE THE FREE CD

INSPIRATIONAL MEDITATIONS

TRACK 1: INTRODUCTION TO MEDITATION

TRACK 2: THE MORNING MEDITATION

The morning meditation has been designed to help you build your self confidence and self appreciation, so you can begin each day in a positive and uplifting way.

TRACK 3: THE EVENING MEDITATION

The evening meditation will remove any tension, stress or anxiety that may have built up during the day and promote complete relaxation and inner peace. Relaxed you will be able to enjoy the evening and sleep soundly and peacefully. Properly rested you will awake refreshed and ready to take on the day ahead with passion and determination.

TRACK 4: THE ENLIGHTENMENT MEDITATION

The enlightenment meditation will take you on a journey of self discovery and learning. Use this meditation to decipher the meaning of any of the quotations or uplifting thoughts contain in this book or to ask your unconscious mind to guide you in any of the present challenges you may be experiencing in your life at the moment.

31 Uplifting Thoughts & Quotations
for

January

1

**A journey of a thousand miles
begins with a single step.**

- Lao-Tzu

 2

**The grass is never greener
on the other side.**

- Garry Malone

 3

**Nothing great was ever
achieved without enthusiasm.**

- Ralph Waldo Emerson

❖ **4** ❖

In the middle of difficulty lies opportunity.
- Albert Einstein

❖ **5** ❖

**Respond intelligently even
to unintelligent treatment.**
- Lao-Tzu

❖ **6** ❖

**Stories are stepping stones on the
path to spiritual enlightenment.**
- Ruth Stotter

7

He who has begun has half done.
- Horace

 8

Effort only fully releases its reward
after a person refuses to quit.
- Napoleon Hill

 9

In the deeper reality beyond space and time,
we may be all members of one body.
- Sir James Jeans

10 ❖

When you were born, you cried and the world rejoiced.
Live your life in such a manner that when you die,
the world cries and you rejoice.

- Traditional Indian Saying

 11 ❖

Never talk about anyone else unless you can
say something positive about them.

- Anon

 12 ❖

Man surrounds himself with images of himself.

- Ralph Waldo Emerson

❖ 13 ❖

**Learning to love yourself is
The Greatest Love of All.** - *George Benson*

❖ 14 ❖

**If thou canst believe, all things are
possible to him that believeth.**

- Mark 9:23

❖ 15 ❖

My friends are my estate.

- Emily Dickinson

❖ **16** ❖

**The only genuine love worthy
of the name is unconditional.**
- John Powell

❖ **17** ❖

Procrastination is the thief of time.
- Edward Young

❖ **18** ❖

**Tis not in mortals to command success,
But we'll do more, we'll deserve it.**
- Joseph Addison

❖ 19 ❖

Even God cannot change the past.
- Agathon

❖ 20 ❖

Tis not too late tomorrow to be brave.
- Dr. John Armstrong

❖ 21 ❖

**Give me somewhere to stand,
and I will move the earth.**

- Archimedes

❖ 22 ❖

Man extols God as omnipresent, omniscient and omnipotent,
Yet he ignores His presence in himself!
God is in the heart of every human being ...
All men are cells in the divine organism.

- Sri Sathya Sai Baba

❖ 23 ❖

If you want to heal the body,
you must first heal the mind.

- Plato

❖ 24 ❖

It's a funny thing about life; if you refuse to accept
anything but the best, you very often get it.

- W. Somerset Maugham

❖ 25 ❖

Know thyself.

- Anon

❖ 26 ❖

Nothing in excess.

- Anon

❖ 27 ❖

**The more alternatives,
the more difficult the choice.**

- Abbe D'Allainval

❖ 28 ❖

Acceptance is magic.

- Anon

❖ 29 ❖

There is only one corner of the Universe you can be
certain of improving and that is your own self.

- Aldous Huxley

❖ 30 ❖

Accept the challenges, so that you
may feel the exhilaration of victory.

- General George S. Patton

❖ 31 ❖

God be in my head,
And in my understanding;

God be in my eyes,
And in my looking;

God be in my mouth,
and in my speaking;

God be in my heart,
And in my thinking;

God be at my end,
And at my departing.

- Anon

28 Uplifting Thoughts & Quotations
for

February

❖ 1 ❖

It is better to wear out than to rust out.
- Bishop Richard Cumberland

❖ 2 ❖

Destiny is not a matter of chance,
it is a matter of choice.
- Oliver Wendell Holmes

❖ 3 ❖

Many receive advice, only the wise profit from it.
- Syrus

4

**All through nature you will find the same law.
First the desire, then the means.**

- Robert Collier

 5

Do everything you said you do with enthusiasm.

- Tom Hopkins

 6

Carpe Diem - Seize the day.

- Horace

❖ 7 ❖

We are always getting ready to live, but never living.
- *Ralph Waldo Emerson*

❖ 8 ❖

Education is the best provision for old age.
- *Aristotle*

❖ 9 ❖

All your dreams can come true,
if you have the courage to pursue them.
- *Walt Disney*

❖ **10** ❖

**The only reward of virtue is virtue;
the only way to have a friend is to be one.**
- Ralph Waldo Emerson

❖ **11** ❖

**More gold has been mined from the thoughts of
men than has ever been taken from the earth.**
- Napoleon Hill

❖ **12** ❖

Love is something eternal.
- Vincent Van Gogh

13

One joy dispels a hundred cares.
- Confucius

 14

**When you come to the end of your rope,
tie a knot and hang on.**
- Franklin D. Roosevelt

 15

**Do not let what you cannot do
interfere with what you can do.**
- John Wooden

❖ **16** ❖

**A diamond is a chunk of coal
that made good under pressure.**

- Anon

❖ **17** ❖

**Most people are about as happy as
they make up their minds to be.**

- Abraham Lincoln

❖ **18** ❖

We boil at different degrees.

- Ralph Waldo Emerson

❖ **19** ❖

**Keep your face to the sunshine and
you won't see the shadows.**
- Helen Keller

❖ **20** ❖

**Though we travel the world over to find the beautiful
we must carry it with us or we find it not.**
- Ralph Waldo Emerson

❖ **21** ❖

**Admonish your friends privately,
but praise them openly.**
- Syrus

22

When nature has work to be done,
she creates a genius to do it.
- Ralph Waldo Emerson

 23

A positive attitude is a little thing
that makes a big difference.
- Anon

 24

I'm a great believer in luck, and I find
the harder I work the more I have of it.
- Thomas Jefferson

❖ 25 ❖

We lie loudest when we lie to ourselves.
- Eric Hoffer

❖ 26 ❖

It's so hard when I have to,
And so easy when I want to.
- Sondra Anice Barnes

❖ 27 ❖

Everything is something I decide to do,
and there is nothing I have to do.
- Denis E. Waitley

❖ 28 ❖

Come to the cliff, he said.
They said, we are afraid.
Come to the cliff, he said.
They came.
He pushed them.
And they flew.

- Goethe

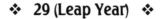
❖ 29 (Leap Year) ❖

All things bright and beautiful,
All creatures great and small,
All things wise and wonderful,
The Lord God made them all.

- Mrs. Alexander

31 Uplifting Thoughts & Quotations
for

March

1

The past does not equal the future.
- Anthony Robbins

2

**To know what is right and not to do it
is the worst form of cowardice.**
- Confucius

3

**Get a good idea and stay with it.
Work at it until it's done, and done right.**
- Walt Disney

4

Hope is a waking dream.
- Aristotle

 5

**The only limit to our realisation of
tomorrow will be our doubts of today.**
- Franklin D. Roosevelt

 6

**You may have to fight a battle
more than once to win it.**
- Margaret Thatcher

❖ 7 ❖

Problems are only opportunities in work clothes.
- Henry J. Kaiser

❖ 8 ❖

**All human beings are born free
and equal in dignity and rights.**
- Universal Declaration of Human Rights

❖ 9 ❖

Absence makes the heart fonder.
- Anon

❖ 10 ❖

Every failure brings with it the
seed of an equivalent success.
- Napoleon Hill

❖ 11 ❖

The worst bankrupt in the world is the
person who has lost his enthusiasm.
- H. W. Arnold

❖ 12 ❖

The mould of a man's fortune is in his own hands.
- Francis Bacon

❖ **13** ❖

**Be happy while your living,
for your a long time dead.**
                                        - Anon

❖ **14** ❖

**God gave you two ears and
only one mouth for a reason.**
                                        - Anon

❖ **15** ❖

Make yourself necessary to someone.
                                - Ralph Waldo Emerson

❖ 16 ❖

**Whether you think you can or
think you can't–you are right.**
- Henry Ford

❖ 17 ❖

Education is not received, it is achieved.
- Anon

❖ 18 ❖

All things are difficult before they are easy.
- Thomas Fuller

❖ 19 ❖

Let brotherly love continue. Remember to welcome
strangers into your homes; There were some who did
that and entertained angels without knowing it.

- James 13:1

❖ 20 ❖

It's not the situation....
It's your reaction to the situation.

- Bob Conklin

❖ 21 ❖

Hitch your wagon to a star.

- Ralph Waldo Emerson

❖ 22 ❖

Hands that help are holier than lips that pray.
- Sri Sathya Sai Baba

❖ 23 ❖

The righteous are like a light shining brightly;
the wicked are like a lamp flickering out.
- Proverbs 13:9

❖ 24 ❖

Arrogance causes nothing but trouble.
It is wiser to ask for advice.
- Proverbs 13:10

❖ **25** ❖

There is always a way if I am committed.
- Anthony Robbins

❖ **26** ❖

Money never starts an idea:
It is the idea that starts the money.
- W.J. Cameron

❖ **27** ❖

Patience means self- suffering.
- Mahatma Ghandi

❖ **28** ❖

**When dealing with people, remember you are not dealing
with creatures of logic, but with creatures of emotion.**
- Dale Carnegie

❖ **29** ❖

**Coming together is a beginning; keeping together
is progress; working together is success.**
- Henry Ford

❖ **30** ❖

Always do more than is required of you.
- General George S. Patton

❖ 31 ❖

Children Learn What They Live

If a child lives with criticism, he learns to condemn.
If a child lives with hostility, he learns to fight.
If a child lives with ridicule, he learns to be shy.
If a child lives with shame, he learns to feel guilty.
If a child lives with tolerance, he learns to be patient.
If a child lives with encouragement, he learns confidence.
If a child lives with praise, he learns to appreciate.
If a child lives with fairness, he learns justice.
If a child lives with security, he learns to have faith.
If a child lives with approval, he learns to like himself.
If a child lives with acceptance and friendship,
He learns to find love in the world.

- Anon

30 Uplifting Thoughts & Quotations
for

April

1

Pursue worthy aims.
- Solon

 2

**A man is not idle because he is absorbed in thought.
There is a visible labour and there is an invisible labour.**
- Victor Hugo

 3

Some defeats are only instalments to victory.
- Jacob A. Riis

❖ 4 ❖

You can heal your life.

- Louise L. Hay

❖ 5 ❖

**Friends do not live in harmony merely,
as some say, but in melody.**

- Henry David Thoreau

❖ 6 ❖

Nothing happens unless first a dream.

- Carl Sandburg

❖ 7 ❖

If a man be gracious and courteous to strangers,
it shows he is a citizen of the world.

- Francis Bacon

❖ 8 ❖

Liberavi animam meam - I have freed my soul.

- St. Bernard: Epistle 371

❖ 9 ❖

Truth is the cry of all, but the game of the few.

- Bishop Berkeley

❖ 10 ❖

**If we all did the things we are capable of doing,
we would literally astound ourselves.**

- Thomas A. Edison

❖ 11 ❖

**Man's mind stretched to a new idea never goes
back to its original dimensions.**

- Oliver Wendell Holmes

❖ 12 ❖

**Words form the thread on which
we string our experiences.**

- Aldous Huxley

❖ 13 ❖

To win...you've got to stay in the game....
                                    - Claude M. Bristol

❖ 14 ❖

What's going on in the inside shows on the outside.

                                    - Earl Nightingale

❖ 15 ❖

To do two things at once is to do neither.
                                    - Publilius Syrus

❖ 16 ❖

Fate tried to conceal him by naming him Smith.
- Oliver Wendell Holmes

❖ 17 ❖

We are slaves to whatever we don't understand.

- Vernon Howard

❖ 18 ❖

**Where you've been is not half as
important as where you're going.**
- Anon

❖ **19** ❖

Treat others as you want them to treat you.
- Luke 6:31

❖ **20** ❖

Plan your work and work your plan.
- Anon

❖ **21** ❖

**Like what you do, if you don't
like it, do something else.**
- Paul Harvey

22 ❖

Vision is the art of seeing things invisible.
- Jonathan Swift

 23 ❖

No man is free who is not master of himself.
- Epictetus

 24 ❖

There are two ways of being happy: we must either diminish our wants or augment our means....

- Benjamin Franklin

❖ **25** ❖

Being good is good business.
- Anita Roddick

❖ **26** ❖

**And the trouble is, if you don't
risk anything, you risk even more.**
- Erica Jong

❖ **27** ❖

**The farther backward you can look,
the farther forward you are likely to see.**
- Winston Churchill

❖ 28 ❖

Man did not weave the web of life,
he is merely a strand in it.
Whatever he does to the web,
he does to himself.

- American Chief Seattle

❖ 29 ❖

Only after the last tree
has been cut down.
Only after the last river
has been poisoned.
Only after the last fish
has been caught.
Only then will you find ....
that money cannot be eaten.

- Cree Indian Prophecy

❖ **30** ❖

It is unwise to pay too much, but it is
worse to pay too little. When you pay
too much, you lose a little money... that is all.
When you pay too little, you sometimes
lose everything, because the thing you
bought was incapable of doing the
things it was bought to do.

The common law of business balance
prohibits paying a little and getting a lot...
It cannot be done. If you deal with the
lowest bidder, it is well to add
something for the risk you run.
And if you do that, you will have
enough to pay for something better.

- John Ruskin

31 Uplifting Thoughts & Quotations
for

May

1

Chance favours the prepared mind.
- Louis Pasteur

 2

Success is simply a matter of luck. Ask any failure.
- Anon

3

Concentrate all your thoughts upon the work at hand.
The sun's rays do not burn until brought to a focus.
- Alexander Graham Bell

❖ 4 ❖

No problem can stand the assault of sustained thinking.
- Voltaire

❖ 5 ❖

**People forget how fast you did a job,
but they remember how well you did it.**
- Howard W. Newton

❖ 6 ❖

**Small opportunities are often
the beginning of great enterprise.**
- Demosthenes

❖ 7 ❖

The day you take complete responsibility
for yourself, the day you stop making any
excuses, that's the day you start to the top.

- Anon

❖ 8 ❖

There is no future in any job. The future
lies in the man who holds the job.

- George Crane

❖ 9 ❖

He conquers who endures.

- Persius

❖ **10** ❖

What force is more potent than love?
- Igor Stravinsky

❖ **11** ❖

When you cease to dream you cease to live.
- Malcolm S. Forbes

❖ **12** ❖

There is no achievement without goals.
- Robert J. McKain

❖ 13 ❖

**The only way to pass any test is
to take the test. It is inevitable.**
-Elder Regal Black Swan

❖ 14 ❖

**Born empty handed, die empty handed.
I witnessed life at it's fullest, empty handed.**
- Marlo Morgan

❖ 15 ❖

Think and grow rich.
- Napoleon Hill

❖ 16 ❖

Every job is a self-portrait of the person who did it.
Autograph your work with excellence.

- Anon.

❖ 17 ❖

Talent may develop in solitude,
but character is developed in society.

- Anon

❖ 18 ❖

When you cease to make a contribution you begin to die.

- Eleanor Roosevelt

❖ **19** ❖

**Reflect upon your present blessings, of which
every man has plenty; not on your past
misfortunes, of which all men have some.**
- Charles Dickens

❖ **20** ❖

Failure is success if we learn from it.
- Malcolm S. Forbes

❖ **21** ❖

**Always do your best. What you plant
now, you will harvest later.**
- Og Mandino

22

If you only care enough for a result,
you will almost certainly attain it.
- William James

 23

The scars you acquire by exercising
courage will never make you feel inferior.
- D. A. Battista

 24

No matter where you go, there you are.
- Buckaroo Banzai

❖ 25 ❖

A laugh's the wisest, easiest answer to all that's queer.
- Herman Melville

❖ 26 ❖

A wise man sometimes changes his mind, but a fool never.
- Arabic Proverb

❖ 27 ❖

The truth is lived, not taught.
- Hermann Hesse

❖ **28** ❖

Only the insecure strive for security.
- Wayne Dyer

❖ **29** ❖

**Our greatest glory is not in never falling,
but in rising every time we fall.**
- Confucius

❖ **30** ❖

What you see is what you get.
- Flip Wilson

❖ 31 ❖

Happy are those who know they are spiritually poor;
the kingdom of heaven belongs to them!
Happy are those who mourn;
God will comfort them!
Happy are those who are humble;
they will receive what God has promised!
Happy are those whose greatest
desire is to do what God requires;
God will satisfy them fully!
Happy are those who are merciful to others;
God will be merciful to them!
Happy are the pure in heart;
they will see God!
Happy are those who work for peace;
God will call them his children!
Happy are those who are persecuted
because they do what God requires;
the kingdom of heaven belongs to them!.

- The Sermon on the Mount

30 Uplifting Thoughts & Quotations
for

June

❖ 1 ❖

Thoughts lead on to purposes; purposes go
forth in action; action form habits; habits
decide character; and character fixes our destiny.

- Tyrone Edwards

❖ 2 ❖

If you don't run your own life,
somebody else will.

- John Atkinson

❖ 3 ❖

The first key to success is deciding
exactly what it is you want in life.

- W. L. Hunt

❖ 4 ❖

Only within yourself exists that other reality for
which you long. I can give you nothing that has not
already its being within yourself. I can throw
open to you no picture gallery but your own soul.

- Herman Hesse

❖ 5 ❖

Success comes to those who
become success conscious.

- Napoleon Hill

❖ 6 ❖

What would you do if you knew
that you could not fail?

- Robert Schuller

❖ 7 ❖

We become what we think about.
- Earl Nightingale

❖ 8 ❖

What goes around comes around.
- The law of Karma

❖ 9 ❖

The power is within you.
- Anon

❖ 10 ❖

The best way to predict the future is to create it.
- Peter Drucker

❖ 11 ❖

**Luck is what happens when
preparation meets opportunity.**
- Elmer Letterman

❖ 12 ❖

**Consideration for others is the basis
of a good life, a good society.**
- Confucius

❖ 13 ❖

**The disciplines you impose on yourself
by writing things down is the first
step towards getting them done.**

-Lee Iacocca

❖ 14 ❖

From little Acorns mighty Oak trees grow.

- Anon

❖ 15 ❖

Together Everyone Achieves More.

- Anon

❖ 16 ❖

**Most good ideas sparkle in simplicity,
so much so that everyone wonders why
no one ever did that before.**

- Estee Lauder

❖ 17 ❖

Communicate with passion, passion persuades.

-Anon

❖ 18 ❖

**You can become anything you want
to be if you put your mind to it.**

- Anon

❖ 19 ❖

Live your life with Passion.
- Anthony Robbins

❖ 20 ❖

**Success is the progressive
realisation of a worthy ideal.**
- Napoleon Hill

❖ 21 ❖

Every Person loves what they are good at.
- Thomas Shadwell

❖ **22** ❖

Give yourself something to work toward—constantly.
- Mary Kay Ash

❖ **23** ❖

When prosperity comes do not use all of it.
- Confucius

❖ **24** ❖

I am the master of my fate; I am the captain of my soul.
- William Ernest Henley

❖ **25** ❖

**The greatest power that a person
possesses is the power to choose.**
- J. Martin Kohe

❖ **26** ❖

The harder the conflict, the more glorious the triumph.
- Thomas Paine

❖ **27** ❖

No pain, No gain.
- Samuel Smiles

❖ 28 ❖

What's right is right, and what's wrong is wrong,
you can't compromise with integrity.

- Anon

❖ 29 ❖

You must constantly ask yourself these questions:
Who am I around?
What are they doing to me?
What have they got me reading?
What have they got me saying?
Where do they have me going?
What do they have me thinking?
And most important, what do they have me becoming?
Then ask yourself the big question:
Is that okay?.

- Jim Rohn

❖ 30 ❖

Ask, and it shall be given.
Seek, and you will find.
Knock, and the door will be opened.

For everyone that asks,
will receive.
And everyone that seeketh,
will find.
And everyone that knocketh,
the door will be opened to them.

- Luke 11:9

31 Uplifting Thoughts & Quotations
for

July

❖ 1 ❖

There can be no transforming of darkness into light and of apathy into movement without emotion.

- Carl Jung

❖ 2 ❖

Winners are grinners.

- Anon

❖ 3 ❖

Life is short, eat dessert first.

- Rita Davenport

4

Children don't lack capacity, only teachers.
- Jim Rohn

 5

Kind words are like honey - sweet to the taste and good for your health.
- Proverbs 16:24

 6

Your will to live can sustain you when you are sick, but if you lose it, your last hope is gone.
- Proverbs 18:14

7 ❖

Invention breeds invention.
- Ralph Waldo Emerson

 8 ❖

I do not seek, I find.
- Pablo Picasso

 9 ❖

Study men, not historians.
- Harry S. Truman

10

There is no God higher than truth.
- Mahatma Gandhi

 11

**We can do no great things -
only small things with great love.**
- Mother Theresa

 12

**Success is the peace of mind
in knowing you did your best.**
- John Wooden

13

**The best things in life are yours,
if you can appreciate yourself.**
- Dale Carnegie

 14

**Nothing is particularly hard
if you divide it into small jobs.**
- Henry Ford

 15

If youth knew; if age could.
- Henri Estienne

❖ 16 ❖

**Formal education will make you a living.
Self-education will make you a fortune.**

- Jim Rohn

❖ 17 ❖

Don't try to talk sense to a fool; he can't appreciate it.

- Proverbs 23:9

❖ 18 ❖

Don't let them steal your energy.

- Adele Malone

❖ **19** ❖

**Nourish the mind like you would your body.
The mind cannot survive on junk food.**
- Jim Rohn

❖ **20** ❖

We are wiser than we know.
- Ralph Waldo Emerson

❖ **21** ❖

In skating over thin ice, our safety is in our speed.
- Ralph Waldo Emerson

❖ **22** ❖

The greatest tragedy is when a person goes to their grave with their music still in them.
- Oliver Wendell Holmes

❖ **23** ❖

If you pay attention when you are corrected, you are wise.
- Proverbs 15:31

❖ **24** ❖

Love the one your with.
- Anon

25

The reward of a thing well done,is to have done it.
- Ralph Waldo Emerson

 26

Challenges are opportunities to learn and grow.
- Anon

 27

**Try not to become a man of success
but rather a man of value.**
- Albert Einstein

❖ **28** ❖

Imagination is more important than knowledge.
- Albert Einstein

❖ **29** ❖

**Am I not destroying my enemies
when I make friends of them?**
- Abraham Lincoln

❖ **30** ❖

**Tact is the art of making a point
without making an enemy.**
- Howard W. Newton

31 ❖

If you continue doing what you've been doing,
You will continue to get the same results.

If you want to change the results you are getting,
You must change what you are doing.

- Garry Malone

31 Uplifting Thoughts & Quotations
for

August

1

Tact: is the ability to describe
others as they see themselves.
- Abraham Lincoln

 2

The actions of men are the best
interpreters of their thoughts.
- John Locke

 3

Riches will do you no good on the day you
face death, but honesty can save your life.
- Proverbs 11:4

4

The best revenge is massive success.
- Frank Sinatra

 5

Nothing has yet been said that's not been said before.
- Terence

❖ **6** ❖

**One of the greatest mistakes in life is
to fear continually you will make one.**
- Anon

❖ 7 ❖

The man who leaves money to charity in his will is
only giving away what no longer belongs to him.

- Voltaire

❖ 8 ❖

Repeat anything often enough
and it will start to become you.

- Tom Hopkins

❖ 9 ❖

Don't serve time, make time serve you.

- Willie Sutton

❖ 10 ❖

Success is a journey not a destination.
- Anon

❖ 11 ❖

**Things may come to those who wait , but
only the things left by those who hustle.**
- Abraham Lincoln

❖ 12 ❖

**Example is not the main thing in
influencing others. It is the only thing.**
- Albert Schweitzer

13

**The louder he talked of his honour,
the faster we counted our spoons.**
- Ralph Waldo Emerson

 14

**Ability may take you to the top, but it
takes character to keep you there.**
- John Wooden

 15

I do not pray for success. I ask for faithfulness.
- Mother Theresa

❖ 16 ❖

Silence is the ultimate weapon of power.
- Charles De Gaulle

❖ 17 ❖

Pennies do not come from heaven.
They have to be earned here on earth.
- Margaret Thatcher

❖ 18 ❖

The buck stops here.
- Harry S. Truman

❖ 19 ❖

I thank God for my handicaps, for through them,
I have found myself, my work, and my God.
- Helen Keller

❖ 20 ❖

Nothing astonishes men so much as
common-sense and plain dealing.
- Ralph Waldo Emerson

❖ 21 ❖

Kind words bring life,
but cruel words crush your spirit.
- Proverbs 15:4

22 ❖

You are where you are today
because you've chosen to be there.
- Harry Browne

 23 ❖

I always tried to turn every
disaster into an opportunity.
- John D. Rockefeller

 24 ❖

If I can imagine it, I can achieve it.
- Anthony Robbins

❖   25   ❖

Choosing to live your life by your own choice
is the greatest freedom you will ever have.

- Shad Helmstetter

❖   26   ❖

The start of an argument is like the first break
in a dam; stop it before it goes any further.

- Proverbs 17:14

❖   27   ❖

Being cheerful keeps you healthy. It is
a slow death to be gloomy all the time.

- Proverbs 17:22

28

Failure to plan means planning to fail.
                                    - Brian Tracy

 29

Your rewards will be determined by the extent
of your contribution, that is your service to others.
                                    - Earl Nightingale

 30

Act boldly and unseen forces will come to your aid.
                                    - Brian Tracy

❖ 31 ❖

Is it so bad, to be misunderstood?
Pythagoras was misunderstood,
and Socrates, and Jesus, and Luther,
and Copernicus, and Galileo, and
Newton, and every pure and wise
spirit that ever took flesh.
To be great is to be misunderstood.

- Ralph Waldo Emerson

30 Uplifting Thoughts & Quotations
for

September

❖ 1 ❖

Friendship can be invited but not commanded.
- Anon

❖ 2 ❖

Sometimes if you want to see a change for the better, you have to take things into your own hands.
- Clint Eastwood

❖ 3 ❖

Little minds attain and are subdued by misfortunes; but great minds rise above them.
- Washington Irving

❖ **4** ❖

**The secret of success in life is for a man to
be ready for his opportunity when it comes.**
- Benjamin Disraeli

❖ **5** ❖

**Excellence means when a man or a woman
asks of himself more than others do.**
- Ortega Y. Gasset

❖ **6** ❖

**If you refuse good advice, you are asking
for trouble; follow it and you are safe.**
- Proverbs 13:13

7 ❖

There's a way to do it better...find it.
- Thomas A. Edison

 8 ❖

Life is largely a matter of expectation.
- Horace

 9 ❖

Do what you fear and fear disappears.
- David Joseph Schwartz

❖ 10 ❖

It is not how much we have,
but how much we enjoy....
- Charles H. Spurgeon

❖ 11 ❖

Fear makes strangers of people who should be friends.
- Shirley MacLaine

❖ 12 ❖

Growth means change and change involves risks,
stepping from the known to the unknown.
- George Shinn

❖ **13** ❖

We first make our habits,
and then our habits make us.
- John Dryden

❖ **14** ❖

Rather fail with honour than succeed by fraud.
- Sophocles

❖ **15** ❖

Good thoughts bear good fruit,
bad thoughts bear bad fruit.
- James Allen

❖ 16 ❖

Live every second.

- Micheal Landon

❖ 17 ❖

A lie is sometimes easier to tell than the truth, but the consequences are always harder to live with.

- Molly Malone aged 10

❖ 18 ❖

Success seems to be connected with action. Successful men keep moving. They make mistakes, but they don't quit.

- Conrad Hilton

❖ 19 ❖

A man is not finished when he's defeated;
he's finished when he quits.
- Richard M. Nixon

❖ 20 ❖

Knowledge is power.
- Thomas Hobbes

❖ 21 ❖

The only lack or limitation is in your own mind.
- N. H. Moos

❖ **22** ❖

You must pay the price if you
wish to secure the blessing.
- Andrew Jackson

❖ **23** ❖

All doors open to courtesy.
- Thomas Fuller

❖ **24** ❖

We have forty million reasons for failure,
but not a single excuse.
- Rudyard Kipling

25

**Genius is the ability to reduce
the complicated to the simple.**
- C. W. Ceram

 26

**Relentless, repetitive self talk
is what changes our self image.**
- Denis E. Waitley

 27

Truth is reality.
- Mary Caroline Richards

❖ **28** ❖

You have to think big to be big.
- Claude M. Bristol

❖ **29** ❖

**For every force,
there is a counter force.
For every negative,
there is a positive.
For every action,
there is a reaction.
For every cause,
there is an effect.**
- Grace Speare

❖ **30** ❖

Just for today I will not worry.
Just for today I will not be angry.
Just for today I will do my work honestly.
Just for today I will give
thanks for my many blessings.
Just for today I will be kind
to my neighbour and every living thing.

- Dr. Mikao Usui: 5 Reiki Principles

31 Uplifting Thoughts & Quotations
for

October

❖ 1 ❖

The empires of the future are empires of the mind.
- Sir Winston Churchill

❖ 2 ❖

Love is life... And if you miss love, you miss life.
- Leo Buscaglia

❖ 3 ❖

**Success seems to be largely a matter
of hanging on after others have let go.**
- William Feather

❖ 4 ❖

There is only one religion, the religion of love.
- Sri Sathya Sai Baba

❖ 5 ❖

**Whatever you can do, or dream you can do, begin it.
Boldness has genius, power and magic in it, begin it now.**
- Goethe

❖ 6 ❖

Honesty is the best policy.
- Richard Whately: Archbishop of Dublin

7

The cure for the pain is in the pain.
- Roger Woolger

 8

Come, test, inquire, taste, experience.
- Sri Sathya Sai Baba

 9

**Life without love is like a tree
without blossom and fruit.**
- Kahlil Gibran

❖ 10 ❖

If you have faith as a grain of mustard seed,
you shall say unto this mountain,
remove hence to yonder place, and it shall remove.

- Matthew 17:20

❖ 11 ❖

The more I learn, the more I live.

- Anon

❖ 12 ❖

There is one thing stronger than all the world,
and that is an idea whose time has come.

- Victor Hugo

❖ 13 ❖

Time is our most valuable asset, yet we tend to waste it,
kill it, and spend it rather than invest it.

- Jim Rohn

❖ 14 ❖

Even a child shows what he is by what he does;
you can tell if he is honest and good.

- Proverbs 20:11

❖ 15 ❖

Genius is one percent inspiration and
ninety- nine percent perspiration.

- Thomas A. Edison

❖ 16 ❖

Do not follow where the path may lead. Go instead
where there is no path and leave a trail.
- Anon

❖ 17 ❖

Things turn out the best for the people
who make the best of the way things turn out.
- John Wooden

❖ 18 ❖

Events tend to recur in cycles....
- W Clement Stone

❖ 19 ❖

Expect victory and you make victory.
- *Preston Bradley*

❖ 20 ❖

The uncommon man is merely the common man
thinking and dreaming of success in larger
terms and in more fruitful areas.
- *Melvin Powers*

❖ 21 ❖

Keep company with the wise and you will become wise. If
you make friends with stupid people, you will be ruined.
- *Proverbs 13:20*

❖ **22** ❖

We tend to get what we expect.
- Norman Vincent Peale

❖ **23** ❖

**Failure is only the opportunity
to more intelligently begin again.**
- Henry Ford

❖ **24** ❖

Liberty means responsibility
- George Bernard Shaw

❖ **25** ❖

He is richest who is content with the least....
- Socrates

❖ **26** ❖

**If you don't know where you are going,
any road will get you there.**
- Anon

❖ **27** ❖

Joy comes from using your potential.
- Will Schultz

❖ **28** ❖

What is important is that one strives to achieve a goal.
- Ronald Reagan

❖ **29** ❖

We know what we are,
but know not what we may be.
- William Shakespeare

❖ **30** ❖

Life gives nothing to man without labour
- Horace

❖ 31 ❖

**A new philosophy,
a new way of life,
is not given for nothing.
It has to be paid dearly for,
and only acquired,
with much effort
and great patience.**
- Fyodor Dostoyevsky

30 Uplifting Thoughts & Quotations
for

November

❖ 1 ❖

Life is eternal; and love is immortal; and death is only a horizon; and a horizon is nothing save the limit of our sight.

- Anon

❖ 2 ❖

The worst prison would be a closed heart.

- Pope John Paul II

❖ 3 ❖

A child needs your love most when she deserves it the least.

- Anon

4

We are all here to contribute something unique.
Deep within each of us lies a special gift.
- Anthony Robbins

 5

Nothing is impossible to a willing heart.
- John Heywood

 6

Love conquers all.
- Virgil

❖ 7 ❖

Many things are lost for want of asking.
- English Proverb

❖ 8 ❖

Don't waste your life worrying about the past and
things you cannot change. Live in the present,
when today is gone it will never come again.
- Harriette-Rose Malone aged 9

❖ 9 ❖

Love cures people, both the ones who
give it and the ones who receive it.
- Dr. Karl Menninger

❖   10   ❖

If you thing in positive terms you will get
positive results. likewise if you think in
negative terms you will get negative results.
- Dr. Norman Vincent Peale

❖   11   ❖

Faith is a continuation of reason.
- William Adams

❖   12   ❖

Each is responsible for his own actions.
- H. L. Hunt

❖ 13 ❖

Who is a wise man? He who learns of all men.
- The Talmud

❖ 14 ❖

Old age isn't so bad when you consider the alternative.
- Maurice Chevalier

❖ 15 ❖

Misery acquaints a man with strange bedfellows.
- William Shakespeare

❖ 16 ❖

Appetite comes with eating.
                    - Francois Rabelais

❖ 17 ❖

A cynic is a man who knows the price of everything and the value of nothing.
                    - Oscar Wilde

❖ 18 ❖

With God all things are possible.
                    - Matthew 19:26

❖ **19** ❖

**Art is not a mirror to reflect the world,
but a hammer with which to shape it.**
- Vladimir Mayakovsky

❖ **20** ❖

Cut the ties that bind.
- Phyllis Krystal

❖ **21** ❖

**Everyone complains of their memory, but no
one complains of their judgement.**
- de la Rochefoucauld

❖ 22 ❖

**Even if you're on the right track,
you'll get run over if you just sit there.**
- Will Rogers

❖ 23 ❖

Men for the sake of earning a living forget to live.
- Margaret Fuller

❖ 24 ❖

Never, never, never, never give up.
- Sir Winston Churchill

❖ 25 ❖

We don't know one millionth of
one percent about anything.
- Thomas Edison

❖ 26 ❖

Genius is the ability to put into effect what is
in your mind. There's no other definition of it.
- F.S. Fitzgerald

❖ 27 ❖

No one can make you feel
inferior without your consent.
- Eleanor Roosevelt

❖ **28** ❖

Who, being loved, is poor?
- Oscar Wilde

❖ **29** ❖

**Nothing in the world can take the
place of persistence. Talent will not;
nothing is more common than unsuccesful
men with talent. Genius will not;
unrewarded genius is almost a proverb.
Education is not; the world is full of
educated failures. Persistence and
determination alone are omnipotent.**
- Calvin Coolidge

❖ 30 ❖

When I was a boy of fourteen,
my father was so ignorant
I could hardly stand to
have the old man around.
But when I got to be twenty-one,
I was astonished at how much he
had learned in seven years.

- Mark Twain

31 Uplifting Thoughts & Quotations
for

December

❖ 1 ❖

What matters is not the size of the dog in the fight,
but the size of the fight in the dog.

- Coach Bear Bryant

❖ 2 ❖

The future belongs to those who
believe in the beauty of their dreams.

- Eleanor Roosevelt

❖ 3 ❖

We know what happens to people who stay
in the middle of the road. They get run over.

- Aneurin Bevan

❖ 4 ❖

Unless you try to do something beyond what you
have already mastered, you will never grow.
- Ronald E. Osborn

❖ 5 ❖

What kills a skunk is the publicity it gives itself.
- Abraham Lincoln

❖ 6 ❖

What's going on in the inside shows on the outside.
- Earl Nightingale

❖ 7 ❖

**Stone walls do not a prison make,
nor iron bars a cage.**
- Richard Lovelace

❖ 8 ❖

No man fails who does his best...
- Orison Swett Marden

❖ 9 ❖

**A man without a purpose
is like a ship without a rudder.**
- Thomas Carlyle

❖ 10 ❖

**Who I am is much bigger than
anything that could ever happen to me.**
- Anthony Robbins

❖ 11 ❖

**Gold and silver are tested by fire,
a person's heart is tested by the Lord.**
- Proverbs 17:3

❖ 12 ❖

**Things don't change. You change
your way of looking, that's all.**
- Carlos Castaneda

❖ 13 ❖

He that is without sin among you,
let him cast the first stone.

- John 8:7

❖ 14 ❖

If one sticks too rigidly to ones principles,
one would hardly see anybody.

- Agatha Christie

❖ 15 ❖

Forgive yourself and others so you
may find true love and enlightenment.

- Garry Malone

❖ 16 ❖

At the end of the game the king and
the pawn go into the same bag.

- Proverb

❖ 17 ❖

You are either part of the solution
or part of the problem.

- Eldridge Cleaver

❖ 18 ❖

Pleasure may come of illusion,
but happiness can come only of reality.

- Sebastien Chamfort

❖   **19**   ❖

It won't happen to me is top of
the list of famous last words.
- David Crosby

❖   **20**   ❖

Keep away from people who try to belittle your
ambition. Small people always do that, but the really
great make you feel that you, too, can become great.
- Mark Twain

❖   **21**   ❖

Everything is self-evident.
- Rene Descartes

❖ **22** ❖

**You cannot teach people anything. You can only
help them discover it within themselves.**

- Galileo

❖ **23** ❖

**Choose a job you love, and you
will never work a day in your life.**

- Confucius

❖ **24** ❖

It is more blessed to give than receive

- Acts 20:35

❖ **25** ❖

Glory to God in the highest.
- Luke 2:14

❖ **26** ❖

**If you don't stand for something
you'll fall for anything.**

- Anon

❖ **27** ❖

One man with courage is a majority.
- Andrew Jacks

❖ **28** ❖

It is never too late to be reborn.
- Garry Malone

❖ **29** ❖

Tell your family and friends that you love
and appreciate them before it's too late.
- Garry Malone

❖ **30** ❖

You are the same today that you'll be five
years from now except for two things:
the people you meet and the books you read.
- Mac McMillan

❖ 31 ❖

**First heal yourself,
so you may find
the inner love and strength
to heal your family,
friends and others.**

*- Love & Light
Adele & Garry Malone*

PLEASE HELP US MAKE A DIFFERENCE

Dear Friend,

We are planning to publish a book containing inspirational true life stories. If you have had an experience that has brought comfort, healing, personal change, self-improvement, love or inspiration into your life, and you would like to share your experience with others please send us your story. Whatever has inspired you in the past, we would love to hear about it. It may be your favourite quotation or an experience that has help you to grow, learn, survive, cope with a loss or achieve a goal, desire or ambition.

Together we can inspire others. Your words of inspiration may help save or change a persons life. People are inspired and can relate so much more to real life experiences. Knowing that others have been able to overcome similar problems and challenges can help people find inner strength and peace of mind when they need it most.

We will of course acknowledge all contributors in the book. If you would like to help make a difference please post, fax or email your story to:

Adele & Garry Malone
2 Talbot Avenue, Watford Herts WD1 4AX
Fax: 01923 245181 email: garry.malone@virgin.net

Love & Light - *Adele & Garry Malone*

FREE CD : INSPIRATIONAL MEDITATIONS

The CD which is included free with this book contains the following four tracks. Each meditation is guided by Garry Malone and enhanced with specially composed music.

TRACK 1: INTRODUCTION TO MEDITATION

TRACK 2: THE MORNING MEDITATION

TRACK 3: THE EVENING MEDITATION

TRACK 4: THE ENLIGHTENMENT MEDITATION

WARNING

Each track contains guided imagery, auto hypnosis, auto suggestion and meditation. While listening to any of the three meditations contained on the Free CD you may drift into a light trance. Trance is a natural and safe altered state of awareness.

However for your safety, please do not play or listen to the any track on the CD *Inspirational Meditations* while driving or operating machinery. It is only safe to listen to and play Inspirational Meditations at a time and in a place when you can completely relax without being disturbed.